The Dedalus Press
editor John F. Deane

THE
SHAPE
OF
WATER

Pat Boran

The Dedalus Press
24 The Heath,
Cypress Downs,
Dublin 6W
Ireland

ACKNOWLEDGEMENTS:

Thanks are due to the editors of the following in which a number
of these poems or versions of them originally appeared:

The Atlanta Review (USA); *The Clifden Anthology; Dedalus
Catalogue 1995/6; Extended Wings; The Hexagram (Dublin)*; *Irish
Studies Review; The Irish Times; The Leinster Express; North Dakota
Quarterly; Poetry Canada; Poetry Ireland Review; Potpourri* (USA);
Redoubt (Australia); *The Southern Review* (USA); *Tracks; Towards
Harmony: A Celebration for Tony O'Malley.* 'The Dead Man's
Clothes' appeared in *Poetry.*

Special thanks to Lorelei Harris of RTE Radio 1's *Sunday Miscellany*
where versions of many of these poems were first broadcast, to
Paula Meehan for responses to this manuscript while still a work-in-
progress, and to Theo Dorgan and all at Poetry Ireland for their
generous assistance.

The author gratefully acknowledges receipt of a Bursary in
Literature from the Arts Council in 1995.

ISBN   1 873790 85 6 (paper)
ISBN   1 873790 86 4 (bound)

Cover design by Michael Boran.

Dedalus Press Books are represented and distributed abroad by
Password, 23 New Mount Street, Manchester M4 4DE.

The Dedalus Press receives financial assistance from An Chomhairle
Ealaíon, The Arts Council, Ireland.

for Michael Hartnett

CONTENTS

Plain Song

*If I were called in
To construct a religion
I should make use of water.*

— Philip Larkin, *Water*

ENTRANCE

It's like what happens with water,
a lake, for example,
which you open
slowly with your hands,

when you sigh, unintentionally,
at a concert recital,
and the breath seems
inseparable from the pain:

you're made human again.

A REVELATION

A persistent nibbling sound
coming from the socket by the bed,
as if electricity were a mouse
gnawing at the dark. So up I get and —

afraid to throw the switch — strike a match
then stretch out on the floor to come face to face

with what I am and have been since birth:
positive and negative in equal parts,
the yin/yang drama of my troubled heart
ignorant of but dependant on the earth.

A CONFESSION

Since none of this makes sense,
since memory is a rope,
since you and I are blind,
I have to confess:

I walked. When I thought
the earth at my feet
was a road, I walked
till I came to the shore

and I spent the night there
listening to water,
exposed to starlight
millions of years old.

2.

Winter was a child burial,
spring a silent meal,
summer
a room full of distractions.

For how many hundred years
have painters turned to a vase like this,
to the light filtering through petals
to describe the world?

Renoir's and van Gogh's
simple flowers in a simple bowl.
You are painting now, again,
to fill the space.

3.

In those early days I too
chose silence. It seemed, at first,
more honest than forcing words
after which — more silence.

But these nights the door stands
open between opposite worlds:
one in which I am still your man
and am content to be,

but another in which an unnamed boat,
untied from its mooring rope,
drifts out of harbour
and into uncertainty.

FOR MY GOLDFISH, VALENTINE

Such enormous sadness
in such a tiny world.
And, looking down at you
in the water clouded
by your flaking scales,
I wonder if my impulse
to take you home
last Valentine's Day
(following a goldfish dream)
was not just a desire
to share my tenancy
of these dusk-facing rooms
under winter's hold.

That dream of gold.

You can imagine how it took me
back into my own smaller body
and bigger, child's imagination
when I found you too incarnate
in an earlier form.
As the lama recognises
his master in a child,
entering the pet shop
I knew you then at once —
the golden fish who swam
in the lens of my parents' house,
in the lens of my childhood,
before floating up one day

to leave that world as I too
left that world, as you
soon again must leave.

Today in the meantime
you look out at me
with the same bewildered eyes,
mouthing the same mute syllable,
the eternal Om that says
nothing changes:

Lead becomes gold and gold lead.
A child will be god when god is dead.

Soon I will recognise your replacement.

PLAINSONG

Even bishops dream of fruit,
angels are drawn to abandoned cars,
and a siren beyond the harbour
calls me to prayer

in a church I had forgotten,
the church of the truth about absence,
the church where stars
smother in the ashes of the sky.

A dangling gantry chain
provides the first tentative notes,
like some creaking shutter opened
to all I hide from:

the suspicion that love includes loss,
the suspicion that those who leave remain,
the suspicion that God is a one-armed man
trying to signal *begin.*

So, let me begin. Let me awake
here in the church of this moment;
no matter that I have lain down
in a field of tongues

let me stand here at the harbour's edge
until gulls come swooping overhead,
screeching into the infinite vaults
our plain song.

CREDO

I believe in a moment where things
come into themselves and everything
before and after is a kind of fading.
I believe, most days, in words
(as I might in diamonds) but
I try them between my teeth before I buy them.

I believe in truth, insofar
as it is a word with an almost
infinite number of synonyms
(though I can seldom think of any
and when I can am inclined to think
they're probably just something I've invented).

On a more sanguine note
I believe I may be dangerous
(to myself as much as to others),
inclined as I am to self-belief —
and this despite the evidence —
though when alone I've been known to compromise.

I believe in making deals,
in foreign influence, new ideas,
in changing minds, too — my own especially.
I believe in love and sex
and children, if they believe
in me. But this could be wishful thinking.

Truths and Rights? Well, these few here
appear self-evident, as they say:
life and the various pursuits.
Otherwise known as loss.
This I believe the ultimate truth:
the liberty to permit oneself to lose.

In the roundness of the planet
(for practical purposes), in life and art
as electromagnetic waves across the surface.
Of something unknown. This I believe.
And in this planet in my absence,
despite Berkeley's seductive philosophy.

In the future, therefore, though English
has evolved no tense for it
as if somehow doubting its existence.
So it would seem that I believe
against the odds, against the words.
But I believe. Witness my belief.

I believe in things other,
things external, in history,
but in something like its opposite, too:
a time unmeasured by events,
where clocks are works of naive art
like milk bottles left out beneath the moon.

I believe in a kind of Zen that says
dim the light to find the stars,
and in the little doll, the pupil, of the eye.
In rhyme, sometimes. I like the slow
almost wary fall of a word to its echo,
but I also like half-pairs, surprise —

though some warning might have helped
to make it easier when you left
last week. Though equally it might not.
If life's a relay, not a race,
doesn't that somehow help to explain
why progress is so often felt as loss?

Always back to loss. Still I believe
it is the handshake that makes the best
and most positive symbol of the human
(though I also rate the kiss
and, in recent times, the Mexican wave;
superstrings, not cause-and-effect chains).

In short (and what else is there?)
I believe the only real prayer
is a list, not of requests but of beliefs;
and this phenomenon of naming
is just another form of breathing
that reminds me how to be and how to leave.

THE SEA

Mermaids on the rocks,
sirens from the shore,
and a bird's dark shadow
cast over the sea.

I am out again on the sea.

And it is out here the octopus wrestles
with air, out here red crabs
scuttle round in circles,
like demented ticket-checkers

going nowhere. And then the quiet,

the sea like silk being torn
as the bird wrenches his new prey
out into sky. It must mean something
that this is how we dream the spirit leaves.

OFFERINGS

skin
hair
breath
teeth

nails
snot
spit
sperm

piss
shit
puke
puss

blood
sweat
dandruff
tears

words

THEY SAY

The gun dog stole the master's gun
and tried to bury it in the garden,
which might explain the noise.

For something woke the entire household
eventually bringing the master himself
from his book-lined study in his nightshirt

and hob-nailed boots — somnambulist
of the quiet hours — clutching air
then stepping out, cautiously,

cautiously, beyond

the porch-light of language.

WORDS

The answering machine
meets my arrival
with unblinking eye.
No word. Now even your voice
evades my traps.

*

Fintan the goldfish,
recently bereaved,
swims round in his world
of light, transparency,
searching for his shadow.

*

Turned sideways, the books,
face to face, square up,
insisting on their versions
of the same old story:
your life, my life.

*

The wine-coloured bedspread
contoured like an ocean;
the wind in the trees;
and your absence... These nights
I flounder not swim.

*

The *pièce de résistance?*
Has to be this cup
with your lip-prints on it,
a tea-leafed shell
I hold to my ear.

*

Calling your name
in laneways only alcohol
knows the way back to.
Every cat knows you now.
Wild dogs remember me.

*

The hearth is always bare
in portraits of the Virgin
to signify virginity.
In mine a fire rages.
I'm burning your love letters.

*

My clothes on the floor,
my body in a twist,
my heart turning over and over
the same old question: whose
words are these anyhow?

*

The keyboard and mouse.
Or this old journal and pen.
At last, if only with fingers,
with fingertips, I'm feeling
for you again.

MOON STREET

It's a minute to, a minute past,
but always the night of the sky,
the waxing or waning or full moon
here on Moon Street,

where every key fits every lock,
every heart is open or broken,
and posters of missing household pets
turn the railway station into a gallery

of loss. What's there to lose?
Come on, there's a party tonight.
Music waits to be released.
The windows are large enough to view

whole sweeps of sky, whole dusty
constellations too long swept aside.
Birds are singing when you arrive,
dancing, or exhausted, in Moon Street.

2.

In Moon Street when you meet she cries,
not on seeing you, but on not seeing
herself, as if a cloud had passed over
some taken-for-granted sphere, leaving

an inexplicable absence in the cosmos,
a strange wavering of otherwise perfect orbits.
But always you can feel that pull,
like the sensation of crossing someone's grave.

Moon Street. Could have called it
Ex-Girlfriend Street, but didn't.
Who could live there were there not
at least some small respite from ghostly visits?

3.

To give oneself completely
isn't wise. But wisdom isn't in it.
More footsteps have taken you to Moon Street
than dreams have shown you moons,

because you get there not by dreaming
but by walking in the wind or cold, or calm,
sometimes having washed, more often than not
ragged, worn and tired. You never realise

where you are going until you get there,
where nothing is planned, nothing is known,
and you're drawn back into the heart's old orbits,
tiny as a grain, massive as a moon.

A CREATION MYTH

The story goes that Wheeler stepped outside,
as is the rule. Great physicist or not,
when you're having dinner at Lothar Nordheim's
you find that leptons, bosons, quarks and whatnot

tend to dominate. It's a relief
when someone suggests a party game. 'The door,
Mr Wheeler. Twenty questions. I believe
everyone knows, as it were, the score.'

Laughter. Wheeler's exit. A puff of smoke.
(I always imagine him smoking in the yard.
Great physicists or not, we're all plain folk
in sudden darkness where any light's a star

and stars mean company.) But what was he thinking of
as it dawned on him they hadn't called him back,
and time was fizzling out like the red dwarf
of his cigarette fading in the dark,

leaving him alone there with his god?
Or just alone… Time to go back inside.
But, as soon as he stepped in, the room seemed odd —
though it might have been the fact that he'd been miles

and years away, and had now to begin
all over, like some astronaut returned
to planet Earth and to these strange beings
who were, he knew — he told himself — his friends.

'Is it animal?' No. 'Is it vegetable?' He'd begun
at least and, in the beginning anyway,
the others answered normally, but then one —
a colleague — faltered, couldn't seem to say,

for sure, yes or no, as if somehow
she didn't know herself! And that smoke again.
Now it doesn't take a physicist to know
when something's not quite right. Still, being trained

in logic means you don't like to concede,
so by the time he asked, 'Is it a cloud?'
he already knew that's what it had to be,
and nothing else. And even as the crowd

composed themselves and started to explain
the joke — how they'd agreed not to consult
but to play by ear — for Wheeler it was plain:
expectation determines the result.

THE TRUTH IS FAR FROM OBVIOUS

Plato had big feet,
Socrates had haemorrhoids,
and Euclid liked nothing better
than getting drunk.

And Judas betrayed Jesus
out of a need for forgiveness,
and Hitler was
a human baby once.

?

It is late now, and the truth
is far from obvious. Popes
are mixing acid in the next room
for the poor.

Make them real or they'll haunt you —
Bigfoot, Pileman, Pisshead.
Left in the shadows, their shadows
will be yours.

DESERT ISLAND DICK

He was a cartoon character
in some comic, years ago,
bearded, scrawny, desperate,
but with no place to go,

obviously, except around.
Which is precisely what they did,
those footprints in the sand
that might have belonged to someone else

had they not led to where he sat
beneath the only coconut,
the only palm tree,
the only sky. One childhood night

I actually became him,
looking up at the stars,
listening to the ocean
of the only words I could remember —

no *Oxford English Dictionary*,
no Shakespeare or Bible then —
just the names of imagined characters:
my own, my family's, my friends'.

THE NON-EXISTENT KNIGHT
(After a painting of the same name by Tony O'Malley)

I'm three, or thirty maybe, but the dark
is a breezy, childhood room made infinite
by conspiracies of movement and light,
refusals of the elements to work
their promised magic. Until the sun comes up
the world remains a curtain drawn across
my eyes, a veil across the nothingness
on which the only light cast comes from us,
from memory — that inner world which burns
but never dies.
              Then here he is,
conjured in all the shades I've grown to miss,
in temporary, shifting, brilliant forms,
reborn in space and time to share this dust,
the patron saint of all my windmills lost.

A TALE

In the forest,
the unicorn and the moon,

both of them
moving through the trees,

as if lost.

At the edge of the forest,
in the village called Thought
(where candles burn through the night
and pendulums swing),

Friedrich Nietzsche,
philosopher,
gives up the ghost.

THE GUIDE

A dog in my dream.
I bend down to pat him
on the head, I bend down to
what-my-own-name-is
him on the head, but he steps
forward on what appears to be
a path, a gravel path,

and my arm must extend
to reach him, then he takes
another and my feet
behind me on the ground
leave the ground
behind.
          Below.
                  Just inches first,
then a couple of feet, my feet,
above the ground, above
the moist perfumed secret earth,
and me floating face-down, stretched out,
limbs like a star's, like the turning
horizontal light the spirit makes
when the chakra doors are open, free,
and then

                he starts to run,
scarcely moving at all at first,
(the way good guides move off, at first,
brisk to inspire confidence,
slow enough so we're never lost),

turning to check once in a while
that I am there, here, following,
to check on the state of my progress
with weightlessness.

               He goes then
as only dogs can really go,
all curiosity, all zest for life,
like Neruda's dog on the Isla Negra,
bounding, bounding, bounding… And I fly,

I fly beside him over ditches,
I fly to the mouth and then back towards the source,
following my reflection in the water,
under bridges, those cathedrals of pure quiet,
before emerging in dark woodlands
where a group of men in uniform
is burying words in unmarked graves —
mother, father, sister, brother, friend —
and lovers groan in their healing labours,
the dogs of earth howling at its moon.

A NOTION OF HORIZON

The beauty of it — a neverland
always within sight
and the poet

crouched over implements
that bring the old gods
down to mortality and earth

like angels and apples
falling in the woods
at dusk

THE PRAYER-JAR

At the bottom of the prayer-jar
was a layer of quiet
so thin it could be missed,
so quiet it might be worn to church.

At the back of the church
you could take, unseen,
the prayer-jar from your pocket,
to collect the sound of people shuffling,

and then go shuffling off back home
through the market visited earlier on,
the clucking of vendors and birds on perches
somewhere in the belly of the prayer-jar.

SONG OF THE FISH PEOPLE

Give us legs and arms
to run and fight and kill,
then give us other skills
to plant and farm.

Give us warm blood
to feel the variations
of temperature, the patience
to untangle bad from good

while the known world spins,
and give us the desire
to create, and the fire
to destroy. And take the fins.

But leave us always tears
that we may not forget
the salty depths
of our formative years.

The Shape of Water

THE SHAPE OF WATER

Four days without it and I'd be dead
and yet I almost never sing its praise
(great evolved life-form that I am) while this shell
washed up on the shore does nothing else.

Like the search for meaning, the search
for the shape of water reveals
only the form of my enquiries:
a bowl, this boat, my body...

Even when I cup it in my hands,
trying to see it for what is,
it takes my own shape, if temporarily;
it gives my own reflection back to me.

So, though we're intimate in the moment,
it seeming to know me as no other,
if water is what I love most —
this thing that has and is my measure —

it is because it sets me free,
because it has no memory.

ᘒ

Precipitation, evaporation, condensation...
home to home to home...

↫

Blue planet the astronauts brought
home to grey cities and green fields;
blue eye of the quest for knowledge
turning in the heavens; blue, blue,
the planet Earth, which is really the planet Water,
a raindrop in the light of distant stars.

↫

You are a distant star, my father
as a young man, and yet your light
persists in the eyes of this old joker
who sits opposite me across the table
where his precious brown-handled knife
lies beside the bread he's always favoured,
sliced, as always, down the middle so that air
might grant it the resistance he admires.

You too are a distant star, my mother
as a young woman, and yet your light,
projected as an image of you strolling
with your five children along the promenade
at Tramore (the long beach) shines still
more than a quarter of a century later
in the eyes of this woman drifting off to sleep
in the flickering lights of fire and television.

The boy on the sand
is king of the castle
till the sea takes it from him
and leaves him a man.

Clepsydra,
the water clock:

precise
forgetting.

Tradition says the inhabitants
of Eket in north Calabar
have a sacred lake,

and that the fish
of that sacred lake
protect their souls.

Perhaps it is
that humans
can not be trusted.

❧

Among Greenland Inuit
spear heads are kept
in seal-shaped boxes

so that, when thrown
in the seal hunt,
they will know the way.

Inside the flesh
of the only fish
I've ever caught:

the smell of ocean,
the taste of ocean…
and the hull of a boat.

❧

Asked to reveal itself,
water says:
                    well,
that noise on the roof
as you sobbed in your beer
and damp wood hissed
and spat in the fire;
last night, remember?

Or, years back, years
ago, the arc
of a 6-year-old's piss
spattering leaves
at the edge of the forest...

Listen, says water,
you can't become
an ocean
without first being rain.

ᡨ

My mother's tears at the hospital
when my sister's quartet of new-borns,
Kate, Sarah, David and Aoife,
commence their ancient, wordless song;

my father's tears at his brother's funeral,
the bucket of clouds in the back yard,
the saucepan of water left out for Miller,
my uncle's dog with the blind eye:

great telescopes and simple mirrors
water leaves for us everywhere
to show the connections between things,
to show us what we really are.

Rain falling in sheets,
pages from the *i ching*
or *Book of Changes;*

small streams
gathering into rivers,
then heading for open sea;

this sea, the same clear element
which composes
two-thirds of my body.

Way of Peace

one's not half two. It's two are halves of one
                                    — e.e. cummings

DIRT

Americans call it dirt — earth,
that is, the soil, not the planet.
Though dirt for me is what dogs do
(what Americans call doggie do),
or it's the scum on collars.

OK. But where's the dirt in love
the Christian Brothers spoke about,
the filth in fucking? Isn't there
a washing clean between lovers,
an absolution of earth-boundedness?

Sometimes growing up seems to be
a digging up of words, a calling
down or even out of meanings:
'This town ain't big enough…'

Though when spacemen (that is to say
astronauts) are floating out in space —
is it Earth they see then there below,

or earth (small 'e'), or simply dirt?
something they have risen from
and would return to: ashes, origin, home.

ISCELLANEOUS ARCHIVAL MATERIAL;
BORAN, PATRICK G.

1. *Main Street, 1971*

I put the flashlamp into my mouth
and I am god or one of the gods
glowing with an orange knowledge
my human cheeks can scarcely contain.
Pumpkin-man, Volcano-Boy.
My head given a whole new life.

And so I know from experience,
how difficult it can be for gods
to speak lest they cremate the world.
Knurrege an ahvish nus — sorry,
Knowledge and advice must be
imparted very carefully.

But who then put all those big words
in that leather-bound book my parents keep
in the sideboard of the sitting room,
a mouth of fire locked with a key?
God? Repeating himself like a drunk!
Or humans like me with flames in their mouths,
fire in their hearts and they burning to tell
the wonder of it, the loneliness of it.

2. In the Star House
(for Peter)

Feigning deep sleep in the shallows
my recent nights have become,
I hear the door open, softly.
Maybe you're drunk.

But as I know how it is
to be you, to see with your eyes,
more than once having found myself
(and always on stairs, for some reason
going down more often than up)
in a body that must be yours,
some kind of astral self —
some future self caught up with,
if briefly — I lie still.

These nights, it seems, are full
of ceremony and magic,
but it is love itself that holds
the flickering lids shut
as my eyeballs turn to trace you
in imagined space.

There's a newness to the quiet
as you climb into your bed,
pull the covers up and stretch
out beneath a midland night,
a night you go ahead into
before me, as older brothers must,
to invent the wheel.

3. Evening News

My old school friend
in a doorway
with a gun.

Somewhere in the bank,
another gun
in a stranger's hand…

What happens next?
It's hard to tell
from this photograph.

For instance
the alarms and sirens
can't even be heard.

But if you listen carefully,
if you look closely,
my friend is saying:

'I've just been born.
There's death in the air.
I have no friends.'

4. Main Street 1996

There's a child on that hook
outside the butcher's shop
every time I pass, a child
dangling like a cup
from its handle.
                        I can't quite see
if the old block inside is gone
or what became of the ceiling-high
refrigerator since they hung
net curtains on the windows
and retired.
                        But someone forgot
the child on the hook outside,
the only thing
about this street that hasn't changed.

5. Why Clocks?

Because the house is a clock,
because every room keeps
time of a different period —

the dark room, childhood,
the living room, teenage;
infancy and old-age, hidden.

And I remember too a clock
where a wooden man and woman
came out when the temperature changed.

'Who's there?' they would say.
'Me,' I'd reply, a young man
still unused to those ancestral spaces,

rooms where a turkey
dripped from the neck
into the same basin each Christmas,

or where mice set off traps
in the still of the night,
while human groans came from the cistern.

Because the steam iron clicks,
a stairboard creaks,
a lock barrel shuts safe into position.

ROUGH

Thieves, and artificial children,
and old men clinging to banisters...
I recognise them; many's the time
I've looked back on, or forward to,
their choreographies.

'It's supposed to be rough,' said
someone's father when I tore my hand
on sandpaper. Now let me say,
if anyone's father tells you that,
there's more than sandpaper on his mind.

And if some thief, or child, mutters
as you pass him in the dripping hall,
or some old guy slouched before a TV set,
the door ajar to his filthy room,
and he red-eyed, barefoot and vested,

says absolutely nothing, stays
mum the way only dads can do,
but peers out from that betrayed beast—
the beached whale of his childhood— then
what he really means to say is
what only that look can explain.

CINEMA

Light is the cause of shadow,
children the cause of death.
And when music is heard
silence is never far off.

The actors are suffering openly
because they never get to be themselves.

Rivers envy stones, stones rivers.

And while the bird on the hippo's back
seems content enough to wait,
the cinema usherette must wonder
what all these lovers of the dark
are hiding from.

LISTENING WIND

He crashed the car through the fence,
got out, calmly, picked up the fence,
turned it on its side, then climbed it,

a ladder into sky.
His parents were there before him,
Marie aged 7, Arthur 5.

Still calm, he took their hands.
A man in sandals and a dinner suit
led them through a door

into a wheat field. The words *listening wind*
came to him for a moment — words! —
then they were gone.

He was led to a garden swing
where he knew he was missing something —
his taunted, earth-bound shadow.

And then he awoke, with a start,
horn blowing, wheels spinning
in mud, wheels spinning in his heart.

CHAIRS

are used to make us sit, not to allow us
to be seated. In this sterile air
who would ever think to disobey
their unvoiced command, their four-square

authority? Just as dumbbells in gyms
test the strength of our devotion
to change, so chairs display our weaknesses:
our need for support, loss of orientation...

The music of the heart is piped through veins.
Until actors arrive the play can't run.
Snails, though always on the road, like poets
never leave home. And so cannot return.

These are our lived-for insights; but when it comes
nothing brings you down to earth like death,
and the wings of cancer angels tipped
with brown-sugared light like cigarettes...

And chairs are used to make us sit and think.
Still after still of the history of chairs
will show the unearthly stillness of their existence,
and ours by extension. So, prepare

for wards like these, long shining corridors,
and chairs, not in unassailable rows
but cooling and moving apart like separate planets,
fading into the luxury of shadow.

And though you feel one now against your arse,
nevertheless it is difficult to believe,
chances are you will be in one, like my friend,
when you would slump, but for it, to your knees.

ENCOUNTER

Sometimes I like you, but I must confess
most of the time, old man, you wear me down,
slumped there in your chair like a sack
of my father's sacred potatoes back home

in a wintry light. And your so-called news,
that 'It is, after all, what they said it would be.'
What is? What all? And who said? Is this why
you asked me to come here, to sit and drink tea

and listen to riddles? And anyway who
do you think you are? — looking like the shade
of my own undead father. And when I offer you
a cigarette you don't even respond, instead

you draw yourself up so the light from behind
makes you appear paper-thin, like a leaf
from a Bible. Then, suddenly, finding strength,
just when I think it must be time to leave,

you're all advice: 'Don't waste your middle years,'
you say. 'Don't treat your life like one big joke.'
But when you finally have to pause for breath,
I strike a match, and once again you're smoke.

PASSPORT

Night time especially
in a foreign place, a foreign language,
I feel like a child.

But then it's always night, somewhere,
and more of the world is foreign
than is known, and words, at best,
slip in and out of meaning
like smugglers and stowaways
passing each other on the docks.

So yet another dark and busy night,
a baby sleeping in its mother's arms,
the cars moving slowly onto the ship,
the sea about to take us to ourselves,
to take us home to where the customs officers
will ask if we have anything to declare,
and unless, like Oscar Wilde, we declare our genius
we may not know who we are standing there
back in the light.

And our passports will offer little help.
We will open them to find kids scowling back,
foreigners who occupy our pasts,
who wear our old clothes and tastes
like uniforms, but refuse to recognise us.
We are all ageing strangers
in their eyes, all under suspicion,
and there is little we can say in our defence.
Some day when we are queuing up at customs,
laden down with Duty Free and bags,
they will barge past without a second glance.

GHOSTS

It is we who are the ghosts.
The ones we call ghosts
are frightened of us. After all
we bustle through their homes,
with our ridiculous sense of urgency
scream our obscene love and pain
as if nothing before had ever been important,
or we slump in our own childhoods, watching
age advance from the horizon. Inexorably.

It is we who are the ghosts.
The ones we call ghosts
have nowhere left to hide.
We have chased them out
beyond their precious moon, or down
to the last shadowed lair of earth
where we follow with torches
to scrutinize their drawings, their prayers
made physical, never noticing our own frail scripts
traced in lines of smoke on the trembling air.

AUTUMN SONG

Autumn returns, and again the trees
shed volumes, all of them seeming
to whisper the same word: *sleep.*

It would be very easy now to sleep
and not to wake again, to lie
in the quiet of this city flat

like an old toy or a bloodstain
and let days creep past. It would be
no negation of the light that's been

to accept the dark's embrace and turn
into myself. And yet last year,
though the leaves eventually turned to pulp

and rain and snow transformed the street,
then vanished, one day I woke to see
a beam of light from this high window

probe the corners, sweep the room,
a beam I felt myself drawn towards
as a seed must feel itself drawn back

into the world.

AGE, LIKE A TRESPASSER

Age, like a trespasser, has crept
into your garden, has found
and sat down to your cigarettes,
exhaling the blue smoke of the future.
Look, now he is playing your guitar,
competent and in no hurry,
and now he is simply regarding the sky
as a man might regard his own hands.

Age, like a trespasser, has crept
into your garden, and the apples
fall from the trees directly,
one by one, into his open bag.
Listen, now against his idle whistling
once more you begin to hear your heart,
and now your dog is barking wildly,
troubled, frightened, by himself.

Age, like a trespasser, has crept
into your garden, and for the first time
you are not alone as the sun goes down,
and familiar colours start to fade.
Now is the time to confront the darkness
though you cannot see the apple blossoms.
Now you must remain quite calm
though from time to time he calls your name.

Age, like a trespasser, has crept
into your garden, and you sleep together
like wolf and sheep, cat and mouse,
perfect and ancient foes.
But in the morning you must rise early
to stand beside his sleeping form.
and recognise those tired old limbs,
before you tiptoe back into your waking life.

'IN HELL, ACCORDING TO GARY LARSON'

In hell, according to Gary Larson,
the maestro will spend eternity
in a room full of gap-toothed yokels,
straw in their hair, banjos on their knees:

And Bach, Shostokovich and Mahler,
and the first song he heard as a boy —
his mother singing Bizet in the kitchen,
shy both in her pain and in her joy —

and his father too the way he hummed those nights
when he had too much to drink, some tune
from his own dead father's lips, the very tune
he ceased to hum the day his fingers died,

the very tune which the night of his own funeral
came for the maestro like a fist of smoke
and dragged him up the chimney into darkness,
away from the attentions of the womenfolk,

beyond the streetlights, up beyond the city,
and down again into some distant room
waiting on the far side of memory
where his father was once again a groom

seated before the piano, and his hands
moved like the hands of a lover,
reaching out, feeling for another,
a New World — all will be forgotten.

For in hell, according to Gary Larson,
the maestro will spend eternity
in a small room full of sweaty yokels:
'Oh! Susanna, don't you cry for me...'

ABANDONED ANATOMY

It should have been, of course, a mere aside,
a pit-stop on my scientific path
around the sleeping but otherwise
undeniable, biological fact
of you.
        Some things are doomed to fail.
Seeing it, I couldn't forget your mouth,
and all those precise anatomical
observations seemed suddenly worn out.

Sigmund Freud and Marilyn Monroe,
Adam, and Eve (the apple of his eye),
the Om, Omagh and Omaha all know,
intuitively, the mouth's a well-known sky
that cannot be described. Their failures prove
the unsayable is the goal of love.

A REASON FOR WALKING

Words when I think,
thoughts when I word.
Hours with this thought only:
Only words,
not what I feel.

The streets offer
not promise, but escape.
Harmony Row, Misery Hill.
Any named place
better than this.

Back home, the summer sheets
an open book, but blank.
But then the light impression
of our bodies, curled up:
the hieroglyph for love.

UNTITLED
(for Kaja Montgomery)

Nothing is mine here
but the symbols of things —
doorways, streetscapes and wings
drawn on the footpath
by a traveller child who,
when the rain washes out his world,
sits up and sings.

HOW TO BE MY HEART

Become elastic,
enjoy the solo sound
as well as harmony.
Enjoy the fall —
don't expect ground.

Never move
but never quite be still.
See life as giving
rather than receiving
though the same blood passes
through your grasp like
rosaries, geometries, bound
infinities of love.

Be practical — work.
Keep the orchestra on course,
but imagine the clouds, the skies
you'll never see.

Learn trust. Don't mutiny
when I wade up to my chest in water.
Don't panic if I succumb to drugs
or drink. Don't sink.
Don't ache at every recollection
of a past populated by grief.
Don't succumb to disbelief.
Don't see only darkness up ahead.

Don't stay in bed all day.
Don't lie down and die.
Be there when I need the heart
to tell the unpalatable truth
or the necessary lie.

And give me the sensation of skydiving
when she so much as
walks into my sight.
Make haemoglobin
while the sun shines.
But keep a little oxygen aside.

BETWEEN THE LINES

Accidental discoveries: coins
Fallen down the backs of easy chairs;
The likeness of a lover, or a friend,
Emerging in a loaf of bread; things
Rising from forgotten places;

And even as you move off towards the future,
Laying what is past, is done, to rest,
Layers of yourself left revealed.

Ignorance is one of the sources of poetry. *

Like a magician who reaches into the hat
On a bad night, his worst in years —
Vera, his assistant, upped and gone,
Even the children noticing his fear —

You find, when you reach into the world,
Occasional if not always blatant signs
Underneath the covers, between the lines.

*Wallace Stevens

ANSWERING MACHIINE

A flashing light will mean I'm not alone.
A moment later maybe I'll hear your voice,
or that of a stranger, or the sound
of someone somewhere having second thoughts,

and hanging up. But at least I'll know it means
that someone thinks about me, now and then,
and whoever they prove or do not prove to be,
at least there is a sort of consolation

in the fact that they send a gift of light,
a sign to welcome me on my return.
You are not alone, it will say, first thing,
the green light of the answering machine.

Or else: *how desperate you've become
for love, the glimmer of surprise,
alone there in the doorway of your room
like a man before an endless, starless sky.*

THE PROMISE
(i.m. Ken Saro-Wiwa)

You sent me letters I never answered,
books I never even opened,
music I neither played nor listened to,
you and your brothers and your sisters,
you sent me maps of your homelands,
pictures of your loved and lost ones,
paintings of your dreams.

I never looked with love
on any of them.

What I was doing it is hard to say:
but as the days shrugged off their names
and the weeks filed past, staggered past
like men in chains, you
were sitting on your bunks among
the gathering spirits of the dead
who say, *Your day will come.*

MURDER

Drumlin country. Passing through
on the Derry bus, it's not so strange —
the scattered towns, the same small houses,
the same sky both sides of the border —
except for the sudden apparition
on a bend in the road of a squad of men,
men in uniforms, and more in the ditch,
scanning the hills for signs of movement,
or staring down their gun barrels
into infinity. And then something else
wrapped in black there by the roadside,
a thing you tell yourself is hay
baled up in plastic and possibly lost
when a trailer took this turn too fast
as the bus is waved on and you look up
at the collective noun for a gathering of crows.

WAY OF PEACE
(i.m. Eamon Keating)

In Adidas runners
and white karate suit
with the simple crest —

a dove round a fist,
Wado Ryu,
the way of peace —

down the Downs,
past the gate house gate,
a chubby druid,

a breathing oak,
a shifting mountain,
following patterns

modelled on monkeys,
eagles and cranes,
stray dogs and dragons,

bird man of Portlaoise,
puff-jowled adder,
dancing bear,

a man in his 60s
somehow
sane enough to play;

and me, 16,
hidden among trees,
glimpsing the way.

'THE DEAD MAN'S CLOTHES'

The dead man's clothes
were willed to the village orphans
so that, those long summer evenings,
he was everywhere,
moving through the fields
until the sun went down,
bloodily.

The villagers loved it, calling
Gretel, Hansel, Romulus,
and watching the old man's shoulder turn
or the big baggy arse
that was his alone come
to a sudden, billowing halt.

Except his wife. Unable
to decide whether this was flattery
or insult, she kept herself
to herself, shut up inside,

while the village orphans
came in from the fields, their hands
reddened from picking berries
and trailing mothballs in the street
like puffs of light.